Pebble® Plus

Hands-On Science Fun

How to Make
BUBBLES

Revised Edition

by Erika L. Shores

Consultant: Ronald Browne, PhD
Department of Elementary & Early Childhood Education
Minnesota State University, Mankato

CAPSTONE PRESS
a capstone imprint

Pebble Plus is published by Capstone Press,
1710 Roe Crest Drive, North Mankato, Minnesota 56003
www.mycapstone.com

Library of Congress Cataloging-in-Publication Data
is available on the Library of Congress website.

ISBN 978-1-5435-0947-2 (library binding)
ISBN 978-1-5435-0953-3 (paperback)
ISBN 978-1-5435-0959-5 (ebook pdf)

Editorial Credits

Marissa Kirkman, editor; Sarah Bennett, designer;
Tracy Cummins, media researcher; Tori Abraham,
production specialist

Photo Credits
Capstone Studio: Karon Dubke, Cover, 3, 4, 5, 7, 9, 11, 13, 15, 17, 19, 21; Shutterstock: Alena Ohneva, Design Element (Bubbles)

Note to Parents and Teachers

The Hands-On Science Fun set supports national science standards related to physical science. This book describes and illustrates how to make soap bubbles. The images support early readers in understanding the text. The repetition of words and phrases helps early readers learn new words. This book also introduces early readers to subject-specific vocabulary words, which are defined in the Glossary section. Early readers may need assistance to read some words and to use the Table of Contents, Glossary, Read More, Internet Sites, Critical Thinking Questions, and Index sections of the book.

Printed in the United States   5542

Table of Contents

Safety Note:
Please ask an adult for help
when making bubbles.

Getting Started

Bubbles float in the sink.
Bubbles pop in a glass
of soda. Mix together simple
ingredients and make
your own super bubbles.

Here's what you need:

1 gallon (4 L)
warm water

1 cup (240 mL)
dish soap

1 tablespoon (15 mL)
glycerin (sold at drugstores)

large plastic tub

spoon

wire coat hanger

drinking straw, potato masher,
spatula, or other utensils
with holes

pipe cleaners

5

Making Bubbles

Pour 1 gallon of warm water into a large plastic tub.

Add 1 cup of dish soap.

Next, add 1 tablespoon
of glycerin.

Slowly stir the mixture.

Try not to make suds.

Let the bubble mixture sit
for two or three days.

Make your own bubble wand
by shaping a wire hanger
into a circle.

Wrap pipe cleaners
around the hanger.

Ask an adult to carry

the tub outside.

Blow lots of bubbles with a straw.

Dip a potato masher into the tub.

Blow through the holes.

Put the hanger into the mixture.

Pull it out slowly. Gently move it through the air.

You may have to try several times before you make a giant bubble.

How Does It Work?

Blowing air can make a thin film of soap stretch. When stretched too far, the film snaps closed. Air trapped inside makes a round bubble.

Bubbles burst when they dry out.
The soapy film gets too thin
and the air inside escapes.
A bubble also breaks when
it touches something dry.

Glossary

burst—to break apart suddenly

escape—to get away from

film—a very thin layer of something

glycerin—a syrupy liquid used in soaps, perfumes, and other products

ingredient—an item used to make something else

mixture—something made up of different things mixed together

Read More

Challoner, Jack. *Maker Lab: 28 Super Cool Projects: Build, Invent, Create, Discover.* New York: DK Publishing, 2016.

Citro, Asia. *The Curious Kid's Science Book: 100+ Creative Hands-On Activities for Ages 4–8.* Woodinville, Wash.: Innovative Press, 2015.

Heinecke, Liz Lee. *Outdoor Science Lab for Kids: 52 Family-Friendly Experiments for the Yard, Garden, Playground, and Park.* Beverly, Mass.: Quarry Books, 2016.

Internet Sites

Use FactHound to find Internet sites related to this book.

Visit *www.facthound.com*

Just type **9781543509472** and go.

 Check out projects, games and lots more at **www.capstonekids.com**

Critical Thinking Questions

1. What happens when a thin film of soap is stretched too far?

2. What can cause bubbles to break?

3. What other items do you think you could use to make bubbles with your bubble mixture?

Index